The Day My Kids Stayed Home
Explaining COVID-19 and the Corona Virus to Your Kids

Written by Adam M. Wallace

Edited by Valentina T. Segovia

Illustrated by Adam Riong

This book is meant to help start a conversation about COVID-19 and what is happening in our world. The first half is a kid friendly explanation of the virus and what we all can do to stay safe. The second half is designed for adults to read before talking with their children so that they can answer any questions that come up. Please learn as much as you can and share it.

Together we can get through this.

This book is dedicated to my Grandma, Mary Ann Wallace. A lifelong educator, she taught kindness and encouragement through how she lived. She never met a stranger and never judged another person. Every time I saw her, she had another "grandkid" that she had adopted and was bringing them a bag full of candy, toys, and books, and insisting that they join her for a meal. Until she passed away, she spent her free time volunteering; oftentimes, teaching children how to read. Everyone she met was family, and every kid deserved a caring adult that would take time to read a book with them.

I miss you.

Once there was a puppy
named Luna. She is a black
dog with a moon shaped white
spot on her chest.

Luna lives with her family: her dog dad, Maui, and her human children. Luna loves her family!

Every morning Luna eats breakfast, then walks her kids to school and drops them off at the playground.

Each afternoon Luna waits at the window, watching
for her humans to come home from school.

She can't wait to play fetch with them and
do tricks for treats!

Luna has a great puppy life!
Walking to school every morning and
playing each afternoon.

But one morning, Luna waited with her leash at the front door. It was time to take her children to school.

The time to leave came and went, but the children did not come to the door.

Luna left the door to look for her children. To her surprise, they were still in their PJ's watching TV!

Luna ran to the window and
looked outside. She could not see
a single child walking to school!
Why was everyone staying inside?

Luna was scared, what was going on? She ran to the couch and jumped onto her sister's lap! The news showed people buying all the food and hand sanitizer at the store!

Luna barked and barked! What was going on? Something must be wrong outside, or they would be going on a walk. Maui came running when he heard Luna barking. The bigger dog licked all the kids' faces and they laughed.

Luna asked her dad why the kids were staying home. Maui told her the whole country was afraid of a new virus called "COVID-19". The family could get sick, so they were staying inside to be safe.

People all around the world were getting sick. Most people felt hot and sweaty. They coughed and coughed. They were so tired from coughing that they just wanted to stay in bed. But after a week or two they felt all better!

Some people got sicker than the rest. Elderly humans and people who were already sick before the virus did not always get better like young and healthy people did.

When people get sick with a virus, their body must learn how to beat it. This is called immunity. If your body has had a virus before, it can defeat it again! Since COVID-19 is brand new, no one has any immunity to it. COVID-19 is also really contagious. That's why so many people are getting sick so quickly.

Maui said "But don't worry. There are plenty of things we can do to beat COVID-19."

Viruses cannot spread on their own. They need us to help them move around. When we high five or shake paws with someone who is sick, the virus sticks to our paws and hands. Even touching a toy after a sick person touches it can spread the virus.

We should always wash our hands (and paws) as much as we can! We should wash them after coming inside the house, before we eat and after going to the bathroom. The more we wash our hands, the harder it is for COVID-19 to make us and others sick!

When we wash our hands, we should scrub them for 20 seconds or more. That is how long it takes to sing the ABC's! Scrub the top, the bottom, under your nails, and everywhere in-between. When you are finished, your hands are clean!

When you finish washing your hands (and paws), dry them off with a clean towel. Bacteria and viruses aren't as tough as we are. They can't live in clean, dry places!

We must stay home for a while to help protect everyone else. Even though we may not get very sick from COVID-19, we might spread it to others who are not so lucky. If we all stay home, the virus won't be able to spread! This will protect people who aren't as strong as you and me.

"That's why my kids are staying home, they are being good citizens and slowing down COVID-19," said Luna as she barked and ran to get a toy.

But when she came back to play, her kids were doing homework on their computers. Since the schools are closed, kids are studying with their teachers and parents online.

Luna asked her Dad, "If the kids must stay inside will we get to go on walks anymore?" Maui barked and said, "We can still go outside but should stay 6 feet away from other people to be careful, this is called social distancing". We must slow the spread of this virus by staying away from others, remember the virus can't spread on its own.

Whenever we cough or sneeze, we should cover our face with an elbow or a tissue to avoid spreading invisible droplets that can carry the virus. And when we blow our snout, make sure to throw the tissue in the trash and wash our paws right away! Even breathing the same air as an infected person may get you sick; that's why we should stay home as much as we can.

"Why is everyone on TV buying masks and toilet paper?" asked Luna. Maui gave Luna a puppy kiss and said that when people are scared sometimes, they do silly things. It is ok to be scared, but we must do our best to do the right things. Luckily, our humans are stocked up on groceries, hand soap, and plenty of puppy treats!

If one of us does get sick, a doctor will tell us if we need to get tested. The test is easy, the doctor just uses a cotton swab to rub inside your nose. If were sick, we will stay home like good citizens to keep our community safe!

Luna asked, "If we get sick with COVID-19, will the doctor give us medicine?"

Her Dad explained that COVID-19, like other viruses, is not treated with antibiotics. The doctor will help us feel better by treating our symptoms, and we will follow the doctor's instructions. For now, we should eat a healthy diet, rest, drinks lots of water and practice social distancing.

Luna wondered if COVID 19 would be around forever. "Will I get to walk my children to school again?"

"In the future there may be a vaccination for COVID-19, just like there is for a lot of other diseases," her Dad explained. Vaccines help our body fight diseases that used to be just as scary as COVID-19 is now. When a lot of people are vaccinated and have immunity, the virus cannot use them to find new people to make sick! This is called "herd immunity". Until then, the more people that stay home and follow their doctor's advice, the sooner things will be back to normal!

Pretty soon we will get back to playing in the yard and going on walks with friends. But until our country's leaders tell us it is ok to go back to school, we will stay home and keep our family and community safe. But don't worry, we will be back to our morning walks in no time!

The End.

For Parents and Big Kids

This book is meant to jumpstart a conversation about COVID-19. If you have questions beyond what Luna and Maui explained, hopefully this section will help you answer them. Remember, COVID-19 is only scary if we make it scary. Take a few minutes to learn about it and then pass the facts on to others.

Together, we will get through this and be better prepared for the next emergency our world faces. Don't stop learning here, talk to your doctor and do some of your own research. This book is not a substitute for medical care or advice. If you don't know where to start check out the references listed at the end.

What is this thing really called?

Disease names describe the conditions and characteristics of the disease. COVID-19 is the name of the disease that is caused by the virus named "Severe Acute Respiratory Syndrome Corona Virus 2" (SARS-CoV-2). The virus is like the corona virus that caused the 2003 SARS outbreak and thus shares a similar name, but to avoid confusion between the two the World Health Organization (WHO) is referring to it as "the COVID-19 virus". Before being named it was termed the "novel coronavirus", novel meaning new.

Where did COVID-19 come from? When did it start?

COVID-19 was first reported in Wuhan, China in December of 2019. The exact origin is still being researched and debated but is thought to be related to a live animal market. When viruses jump from animals to humans it is called "spillover". The first confirmed case of the virus in the United States occurred on January 20th, 2020 in Washington state. Since then the virus has spread to all 50 states in the United States of America. As of March 2020, the COVID-19 virus has spread to six continents and over 150 countries.

What are the signs and symptoms of COVID-19?

At this point in the progression of COVID-19, there is a lot that we don't know. If in doubt, call your doctor and seek out testing and medical advice.

If suffering from the virus you may have all, some or none of the following:

- Headache
- Fatigue
- Sputum production
- Fever
- Dry cough
- Shortness of breath
- Sore throat

Who is at risk?

There have been fewer cases in children and young adults than in older populations. It is thought that age and preexisting medical conditions increase the likelihood of a severe case of COVID-19. Some of the conditions that increase a person's risk include diabetes, cardiovascular or respiratory disease and cancer. Remember even if you don't fall into one of these categories, your friends and family may.

Why is everyone stocking up on toilet paper and hand sanitizer? What should I be doing to be prepared?

During times of crisis or uncertainty people want to regain control in their lives. One easy way to do that is to "stock-up" for what they think is coming. The need to prepare, paired with social cues and non-stop media coverage, has led to panic-buying and things being out of stock. When one person buys six cases of toilet paper, the next person in line at the store is inclined to buy way too much as well. Remember, COVID-19 doesn't cause projectile diarrhea. So, buying all the toilet paper you can find is pretty silly. Instead think about what you need to stock to avoid leaving your house for 2-3 weeks of social distancing; some shelf stable food for you and pets, a board game and a positive mental attitude should do it.

I've heard that COVID-19 isn't any more dangerous than the flu, so why should we be worried?

The severity of COVID-19 varies from person to person. It is true that many are experiencing mild symptoms that seem like a common cold, and many that are infected with COVID-19 are asymptomatic (infected and contagious but no signs of being sick). As of March 2020, roughly 80% of COVID-19 patients experience a mild illness. The other 20% will require medical care; of them roughly 1/3 will end up needing a ventilator and hospital care. Early studies in China estimated the mortality rate near 3%, but in Italy during March 2020 the rate has been near 9%. We still don't know how bad this will be. The incredibly fast infection rate of COVID-19, and that 20% of patients may need hospital care is what makes it dangerous. This has the potential to be much more serious than standard influenza.

What is the difference between a bacteria and a virus?

Both bacteria and viruses are invisible to the naked eye and cause illness in people, however the two are treated in very different ways. Bacteria are single cell organisms that can live and reproduce on their own. In contrast, viruses are even smaller and are not complete cells or living organisms. Viruses enter healthy cells in other animals (called the host) and then use the host cell to multiply, in the process they can harm the host and cause illness. Bacteria can be treated with antibiotics. Antibiotics do not do anything to viruses like COVID-19. To treat a virus, medical providers may treat the symptoms of it. Vaccines prevent infection from some viruses and anti-viral drugs can lessen the effect of the infection.

What is a corona virus?

Corona Viruses are a family of viruses that all appear similar under a microscope. The name comes from the Latin word Corona which means crown, under a microscope the viruses look like there is a crown on top. Corona viruses can infect animals and people, and sometimes they spillover from animals and into humans. Each virus causes a different disease, with different severity and infectivity. Other corona viruses that you may have heard of include MERS (Middle East Respiratory Syndrome) and SARS (Severe Acute Respiratory Syndrome).

Why aren't doctors prescribing antibiotics for patients with COVID-19?

Antibiotics do not treat viruses! As of March 2020, there is no treatment to "cure" COVID-19. Doctors can help to treat the symptoms, which means they aren't curing you, but they can help your body feel better and be stronger. Examples of this include cough suppressants if you have a cough, or acetaminophen if you have a fever. For severe patients, supplemental oxygen or using a ventilator (a machine that blows air into the lungs to help you breath) can help them survive and recover faster.

Will the flu shot help against COVID-19?

Not at all. The flu shot provides protection against several strains of influenza. Since COVID-19 is not a strain of influenza, the flu shot offers no protection. At this point social distancing and good hygiene are your best defenses.

How does the test for COVID-19 work?

In the United States most tests are using either nasal or throat swabs. A medical technician will swab inside your mouth or nose with a cotton swab, and then send the sample to a lab for testing. The lab sequences the DNA of the sample (like what they do for a family tree/ancestry test) and looks for virus matches. COVID-19 has about 30,000 nucleotides which are the basic structure of DNA, the test looks for roughly 100 of them that identify the virus. Faster tests that don't need a lab are being developed for use in the United States.

What does it mean to be "immune" to a virus, or "have immunity"?

When you have a virus, your body responds by generating antibodies which are a special protein in your blood. Antibodies attach to the protein within the virus and signal white blood cells to destroy it. After your body has destroyed the viral infection, some of those antibodies remain in your body. The next time you are exposed to the virus those remaining antibodies help your body quickly defeat it or prevent infection. We are still not sure if you can be immune to COVID-19, but scientists are working to determine if after infection you retain an immunity to COVID-19.

What is herd immunity?

A key concept of public health is "herd immunity". For a virus to spread, people must become infected and pass the virus to others. If everyone was immune to the virus it would not be able to spread at all, but totally immunity is almost impossible to attain (costly, logistically challenging to get everyone vaccinated, some people have health conditions that make vaccines dangerous). If most of a population is immune, the virus may spread between a few people, but it cannot rapidly spread as there just aren't enough infectible people. When most of the community is immune, the reduced ability to spread protects those that cannot get vaccinated.

Can my pet get sick with COVID-19 or make me sick?

Current research has not found pets that have become infected with COVID-19 or found any animal to person transmission. But there is a lot we don't know; if you become sick, try to avoid contact with your pets. If you cannot avoid your pets, you can minimize their risk by washing your hands and wearing a mask before you interact with them. The CDC recommends always washing your hands after touching any animal.

Why is handwashing recommended?

Since none of us are immune to COVID-19, we must protect ourselves from infection by avoiding the viral particles. Virus particles are invisible to the unaided eye; they are spread by an infected person when they touch an object or cough and breath in an area. After touching anything near an infected person or something others have touched (since you don't know if they are infected) wash your hands. When washing your hands scrub vigorously over all surfaces of your hand using soap and water for at least 20 seconds. This will remove most of the viral particles from you. Avoid touching your eyes, face, or mouth before washing your hands. If a sink is unavailable hand sanitizer with 60% or higher alcohol can be used. There is no need to buy/use hand sanitizer if you have access to soap and a sink, save hand sanitizer for when you are on the go.

What is "social distancing" and why are we doing it?

Right now, no one has immunity to COVID-19 since it is a new virus. To protect people from getting infected the only thing we can do is avoid exposure. Each time you go outside and get near a person or touch something that others have touched you run the risk of being exposed to COVID-19. By closing restaurants and schools and asking people to stay indoors, the government is trying to stop people from getting infected. Even if you are not worried getting sick, remember each time you leave the house you are potentially exposing others. Social distancing is more about protecting your vulnerable family and neighbors than it is about protecting you.

How can I disinfect things?

We still don't know exactly how long the virus that causes COVID-19 can live outside of a host. We think that it survives as an aerosol as long as three hours, up to four hours on copper, and 24 hours on cardboard. On hard surfaces it lasts even longer - possibly, up to three days on steel or plastic. Clean surfaces with soap and water, for hard surfaces disinfectant products can be used. A diluted bleach mixture of 5 tablespoons per gallon water (20 ml bleach to 1 liter water) is an effective disinfectant. It is impractical for most people to disinfect the air. Opening windows for extra ventilation or meeting outside may reduce the concentration of virus particles but the only real protection is to stay inside and practice social distancing. If you must leave the house staying 6 feet or more away from others can reduce the risk of virus transmission.

Flatten the Curve

There are still many unknowns surrounding COVID-19, but governments around the world are implementing a strategy designed to "flatten the curve" of infection and save lives. The phrase "flatten the curve" is being repeated in the news and online, but not everyone entirely understands why this policy is so important.

COVID-19 is highly contagious and has demonstrated its ability to rapidly spread through a population and around the world. Italy in March 2020 is the perfect case study to show why we must slow down the spread of the virus. On February 15th the country had 3 cases. Within a few weeks, it had more than 50,000 cases. Roughly 20% of the cases were severe enough to require hospitalization which equates to over 10,000 people needing a hospital bed and respiratory care. Italy ran out of medical equipment and lacked enough hospital staff to care for patients. The military had to be deployed to manage the massive quantity of bodies overwhelming the country's morgues. Elderly patients diagnosed with COVID-19 were sent to hospice rather than hospitals that lacked room to care for them and hospitals triaged younger patients over elderly ones. Italy has 3.2 hospitals beds for every 1000 people, the United States has 2.8.

The chart to the right repsresents two scenarios; in purple the uncontrolled virus is spread by people ignoring government guidance and the tan curve shows the result of millions of citizens responsibilly social distancing. The red line represents the nation's healthcare capacity (the number of doctors, beds, ventilators, masks, gloves, body bags). If the virus accelerates too quickly the healthcare system will be overhwelmed, and more people will die.

Social distancing is our best defense to slow down the spread of COVID-19. Every time someone ignores social distancing or isolation guidance and leaves their home unnecessarily, they run the risk of contracting or spreading COVID-19. Even if you are in a "low risk" age group or fitness category, think about all of those that are at a higher risk. Every time you go out you put someone's grandparent or sick child at risk. COVID-19 is going to kill people, it's up to every one of us to do our part.

Stay home and socially distance whenever possible, it will "flatten the curve" and save lives.

References and More Information

We are living through a constantly changing health emergency, and sadly a lot of misinformation is being spread online and around the world. Below are a few reliable sources that you can get more information from, and please don't bury your head in the sand. Listen to the radio, watch and read the news and follow the guidance given by government and medical leaders.

Centers for Disease Control
cdc.gov/coronavirus

World Health Organization
who.int/emergencies/diseases/novel-coronavirus-2019

Harvard Medical School – Coronavirus Research Center
https://www.health.harvard.edu/diseases-and-conditions/coronavirus-resource-center

New England Journal of Medicine
https://www.nejm.org/coronavirus

Khan Academy – Easy to Understand Video Lessons
https://www.khanacademy.org/science/biology/bacteria-archaea
https://www.khanacademy.org/science/biology/biology-of-viruses

A Global Medicine Doctor's new take on Covid-19 by Dr Ben LaBrot – Medium.Com
https://medium.com/@DoctorBen/a-global-medicine-doctors-new-take-on-covid-19-347c473ab0b5

ACKNOWLEDGMENTS

This book would not have been possible without the support of many amazing people.

Val, thank you for editing it a hundred times and tolerating the late nights and nerdiness! You always are there to support me, I couldn't have done it without you. I love you.

Ben, you sparked my interest in medicine years ago and have been supporting me the entire time. Thanks for being my sounding board on this and helping to get this project distributed as quickly as possible. Stay safe, you and the Floating Doctors Team are the vanguard for public health.

Stocker, my (almost) Doctor friend on call. Thanks for editing and revising for me.

Dad, you are probably tired of editing papers for me. But at least we got one published, thank you. You have always had my back.

Mom, thanks for always being there and making sure the book was kid friendly!

Jordan, thank you for putting a doctor's review on this. Thousands around the world are indebted to you for always being on the frontline with a stethoscope in hand.

To everyone else that contributed, thank you!

Help Give Back

10% of the profit generated from "The Day My Kids Stayed Home" will be donated to the Floating Doctors.

Our world is more interconnected now than ever. The rapid spread of COVID-19 from Wuhan China to the entire world is illustrative of the struggle to maintain public health in a globalized world. If any patient, any community, any where in the world is ignored it affects each of us.

The Floating Doctors is a non-profit medical group that provides care for remote communities and is dedicated to the idea that every person deserves medical care. Initially started on sailboat by Dr. Benjamin LaBrot, who realized that over 40% of the world's population lives near the coast and a boat can carry way more medical gear than a backpack. The group is now operating in rural Panama running free clinics in isolated communities. Every day volunteers drive small boats across the ocean and climb mountains to get to villages the world has forgotten.

We don't know where the next pandemic will start, but Floating Doctors will surely be on the frontline. Let's fund them now so they are ready.

Donate now and find out more at the link below.

WWW.FLOATINGDOCTORS.COM

ABOUT THE AUTHOR

Adam Wallace has been an Emergency Medical Technician for 11 years and is currently studying towards a Master's in Public Health at the University of South Florida. Adam is in the United States Air Force and is married to his high-school sweetheart Valentina. Before enlisting he spent three years working and volunteering for the non-profit Floating Doctors providing medical care for remote patients in rural Panama. *The Day My Kids Stayed Home* is his first book; he wrote it to help young kids disrupted by COVID-19 understand what is happening in the world. Luna was his dog as a kid, and Maui is Val and Adam's puppy today.

ABOUT THE ILLUSTRATOR

Adam Riong, a Malaysian illustrator and artist brought the book *The Day My Kids Stayed Home* to life with his illustrations. To see more of Riong's work visit his website: https://www.behance.net/paperpieceproject or instragram.com/adam_paperpiece/

CPSIA information can be obtained
at www.ICGtesting.com
Printed in the USA
LVHW051607010620
657149LV00008B/632